**ABDO**
**Publishing Company**

# Eat Well

GET HEALTHY

Buddy BOOKS
Get Healthy

A Buddy Book by **Sarah Tieck**

# VISIT US AT
### www.abdopublishing.com

Published by ABDO Publishing Company, PO Box 398166, Minneapolis, MN 55439.

Printed in the United States of America, North Mankato, Minnesota.
102011
012012

 PRINTED ON RECYCLED PAPER

Coordinating Series Editor: Rochelle Baltzer
Contributing Editors: Megan M. Gunderson, BreAnn Rumsch, Marcia Zappa
Graphic Design: Jenny Christensen
Cover Photograph: *iStockphoto*: ©iStockphoto.com/kissesfromholland.
Interior Photographs/Illustrations: *Eighth Street Studio* (p. 26); *iStockphoto*: ©iStockphoto.com/AdShooter (p. 11), ©iStockphoto.com/apomares (p. 25), ©iStockphoto.com/ChristopherBernard (p. 25), ©iStockphoto.com/iofoto (p. 5), ©iStockphoto.com/kcline (p. 13), ©iStockphoto.com/kledge (p. 19), ©iStockphoto.com/mantonino (p. 17), ©iStockphoto.com/monkeybusinessimages (p. 23), ©iStockphoto.com/Tomboy2290 (p. 27), ©iStockphoto.com/VikramRaghuvanshi (p. 11); *Shutterstock*: Yuri Arcurs (p. 21), Shpilko Dmitriy (p. 9), Ryan R Fox (p. 27), Rusian Ivantsov (p. 11), Maridav (p. 15), Monkey Business Images (pp. 29, 30), Thomas M Perkins (p. 30), Karen Sarraga (p. 9), Franco Volpato (p. 17); *USDA* (p. 7).

## Library of Congress Cataloging-in-Publication Data

Tieck, Sarah, 1976-
  Eat well / Sarah Tieck.
    p. cm. -- (Get healthy)
  ISBN 978-1-61783-232-1
  1. Nutrition--Juvenile literature. I. Title.
  TX355.T527 2012
  613.2--dc23
                        2011028952

# Table of Contents

# Healthy Living

Your body is amazing! It does thousands of things each day. It lets you run, talk, and think. A healthy body helps you feel good and live well.

In order to be healthy, you must take care of your body. One way to do this is to eat well. So, let's learn more about foods and **nutrients**!

Eating well gives you energy. It also helps your body become stronger.

# Eat This, Drink That

There are five food groups. They are protein, dairy, grains, fruits, and vegetables. To eat well, choose healthy foods from each group. Your body needs **nutrients** from all of them to be healthy.

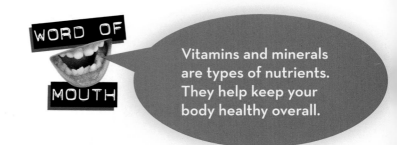

WORD OF MOUTH

Vitamins and minerals are types of nutrients. They help keep your body healthy overall.

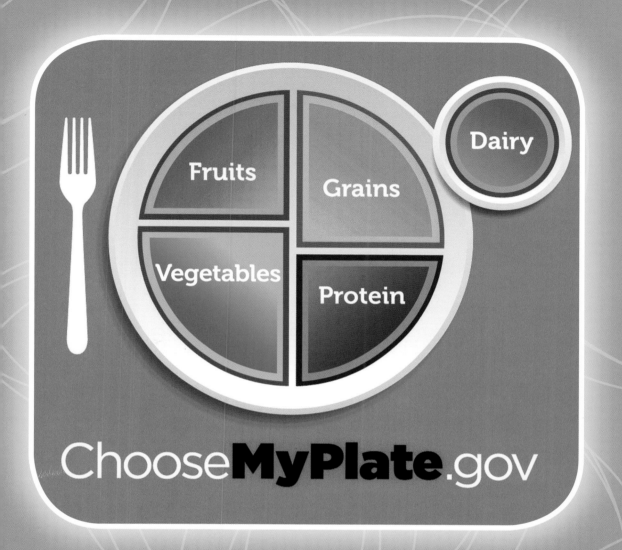

Fruits

Grains

Dairy

Vegetables

Protein

ChooseMyPlate.gov

In 2011, the US government presented MyPlate.
It shows how much of each food group to eat.

# Lean and Strong

Foods in the protein group include meats, seafood, beans, eggs, and nuts. They help your body build and heal bones and **muscles**. Choose meats that are lean, or low in fat.

Foods in the dairy group include milk, cheese, and yogurt. They give your body **nutrients**, such as calcium. This mineral helps your bones grow strong.

WORD OF MOUTH

Most foods in the dairy group are made from cow's milk. But, soy milk and foods made from goat's milk are also included.

Grilled chicken is a healthy lean protein.

Tofu and other foods made from soybeans are good protein sources.

Eating fiber is good for your heart!

WORD OF MOUTH

Your body needs grains for **energy**. The healthiest are whole grains. Oats, whole wheat, and brown rice are whole grains.

Whole grains have fiber, vitamins, and iron. Fiber helps move food through your body. Vitamins help your body make better use of food. And, iron helps keep your blood healthy.

Whole grains come from the whole seeds of plants. White bread (*below*) is made from only part of the seed. So, whole grain bread (*right*) has more nutrients.

Whole grains are in certain breads, oatmeal, and popcorn.

# Just Eat It!

Fruits and vegetables are your friends. Eating them boosts your health. They can be enjoyed raw or cooked.

Different colored fruits and vegetables provide different nutrients. So, eat a rainbow of fruits and vegetables!

**Oranges** have vitamin C. This helps your body heal if you have a cut.

**Asparagus** has B vitamins. These help keep your brain working well.

**Purple grapes** have nutrients that keep your cells healthy.

# Raise Your Glass

When you're thirsty, what do you reach for? Water is one healthy drink. It helps your body use food and get rid of waste.

Another healthy drink is low-fat milk. Milk is a dairy food, so it even gives your body **nutrients**!

Drink soda and fruit punch only as a special treat. They often have unhealthy **ingredients** and a lot of sugar.

Water helps keep your body clean inside and out!

# Freshen Up

When you can, eat foods that come from nature or animals. Limit **processed** foods. These are made in factories. They often have man-made **ingredients**.

Some foods are ready to eat. You can pick an apple right off the tree! Others, such as natural milk, may get a small amount of processing.

Natural cheeses are made from milk with little processing.

Cheese packets in boxed macaroni and cheese are created in factories.

# Look and Learn

Many foods come in packages with labels. Learn about your food by reading its label.

A food's label lists its **ingredients** and **nutrients**. It shows the size of a **serving**. It shows how many servings are in the package. And, it shows the amount of calories in one serving.

You may hear adults talk about counting calories. Calories are used to show how much fuel food will give the body.

**Nutrition Facts**
Serving Size 1 Tablespoon
Servings Per Container

**Amount Per Serving**

**Calories** 110 Calories

**Total Fat** 12g
Saturated Fat 3
Trans Fat 0g
Polyunsatu
Monouns
Cholest
Sodiu

WORD OF MOUTH

Some foods have a long list of ingredients. These foods are more processed than others.

# Cook It Up

Choosing the right foods is only part of eating healthy. The way you cook them also plays a part. Baking, steaming, and grilling are healthy ways to prepare foods.

Other ways of cooking can make a healthy food unhealthy. These include frying food in fat and adding a lot of sugar or salt.

Ask an adult to help you
make a healthy grilled dinner.

# Now and Later

Food is **fuel** for your body. It helps you grow strong. The amount of food you eat is important.

It is unhealthy to eat too little food. A person's body won't have enough fuel or **nutrients**. This can cause a person to get sick or become too thin.

Eating a healthy lunch gives you energy for the day!

Eating too much food is also unhealthy. If you eat more than your body needs, the extra calories may be stored as fat. This can cause weight gain.

Over time, being overweight can lead to serious health problems. These include heart problems and **diabetes**. Make good choices now to keep your body healthy for many years!

Exercise is one way to use up energy from food you eat. But, your body is always working. You use energy even while you sleep!

# Brain Food

## How do you know how much food to eat?

Every person needs different amounts of food. How much you should eat depends on your activity level and size. Children usually need less food than young adults. Eat when your body is hungry. Stop when it feels full, not stuffed.

**The Hunger Scale**

10 Stuffed

7 Full

5 Comfortable

3 Hungry

0 Empty

## Is there such a thing as healthy fat?

Yes! Healthy fats are in foods such as avocados and nuts. These fats are good for your skin and hair. And, they keep your **organs** working well. Fats such as those found in fast food are unhealthy.

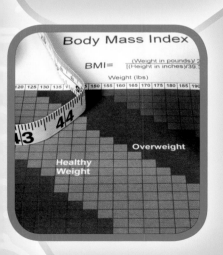

## How do I know if I'm the right weight?

One way people measure healthy weight is with a body mass index (BMI). This number shows whether you are underweight, normal, overweight, or very overweight. Ask an adult or your doctor to find your BMI.

# Making Healthy Choices

Remember that food is **fuel** for your body. Try to eat only when your body is hungry. Before you take a bite, stop and think. What will that food do for your body?

Eating well is just one part of a healthy life. Each positive choice you make will help you stay healthy!

Eating healthy can be easy! Have an apple with your lunch, and add lettuce to your sandwich.

# HEALTHY BODY FILES

## EAT SMART

✔ Fruit, yogurt, and salads are healthy choices at many fast food restaurants.

✔ French fries are okay to eat in small amounts. Try sharing them with a friend or family member!

## SCHOOL COOL

✔ Make your school lunch healthy. Eat your vegetables and drink your milk!

✔ Be sure to eat breakfast before school. Choose eggs, oatmeal, or fruit instead of sweet cereals.

## POWER UP

✔ Choose brown bread instead of white bread. Many brown breads are made with whole grains. The fiber in them makes you feel full longer.

✔ Bring a bottle of water in your backpack!

# Important Words

**diabetes** (deye-uh-BEE-teez) a condition in which the body cannot properly take in normal amounts of sugar or starch.

**energy** (EH-nuhr-jee) the power or ability to do things.

**fuel** (FYOOL) something that provides energy.

**ingredient** (ihn-GREE-dee-uhnt) a part mixed with other parts to make a product.

**muscle** (MUH-suhl) body tissue, or layers of cells, that helps move the body.

**nutrient** (NOO-tree-uhnt) something found in food that living beings take in to live and grow.

**organ** a body part that does a special job. The heart and the lungs are organs.

**process** to change or keep from rotting by using chemicals or machines.

**serving** a unit of measure that gives the suggested amount of food or drink.

# Web Sites

To learn more about eating well, visit ABDO Publishing Company online. Web sites about eating well are featured on our Book Links page. These links are routinely monitored and updated to provide the most current information available.

## www.abdopublishing.com

31

# Index